PICTURE BOOK

CATHOLIC
PRAYERS

Gedaliah Shay

Alpha Zuriel Publishing

Cover design: Anchorage
Editing: Samantha Baines
Imprint: Independently published

Printed in the United States of America

Lord God, grant me the ability to enjoy my rest so that I might be ever fresh and alert to your Love and mercy in my life.

Lord God, enable me to see the face of Christ in my life and in everyone I see

In you, LORD, I take refuge; let me never be put to shame.

Be my Rock and refuge, my secure stronghold; for you are my Rock and fortress.

On you I depend since
birth; from my
mother's womb,
you are my
strength; my hope
in you will never
waver.

I shall sing of your glory every day. I pray thee, Do not cast me aside in my old age; as my strength fails, do not forsake me.

Day after day your acts
of deliverance,
though I cannot
number them all, I
shall always speak
of the
mighty and
glorious works of
the Lord

Please Lord,
Teach me to
understand my
suffering as You
do
and To bear it in
dignity in union
with
You.

Lord Jesus, please alleviate my fears and increase my trust in you.

Lord, If it be
Your holy will,
please restore my
health
to work for Your
glory and honor
and the salvation
of all men.

Mary, help of the sick, pray for me.

The
Lord has done
great things for
me; I am filled
with joy.

I ask that I may
find joy in a
renewed strength
of spirit,
that I may have
good health
through Christ
Jesus

All-powerful
and ever-living
God, in whom I
live and move, I
thank
you and praise
you for giving me
long years, lived
in faith and in
doing good.

Lord Grant that I may
have the loving
support of friends
and relatives, I
will be cheerful in
good
health, and in
poor health, I will
not lose hope.

With the help of your blessing, let me spend my old age giving praise to your name. I ask this through Christ our Lord.

Let me be aware of
your nearness
so that, when I
worry about past
failures, I will
rejoice in your
mercy. I ask
this through Christ
our Lord.

May the Lord
Jesus Christ be
with
me to protect me.

May almighty
God bless me, in
the
name of the
Father, and the
Son, + and the
Holy Spirit.